synaestHesia
Inez Gitzinger-Albrecht

rhythmvision rhythmvision rhythmvision

Impressum

Autorin/Künstlerin: Inez Gitzinger-Albrecht

Edition: Atelier Rhyvis, Europa, Germany Freiburg, 2015
Neuauflage

Austellungskatalog, 2005 KiKi, Freiburg

Kurator : Theo Hofsaess, Freiburg, Germany
Jury: Theo Hofsaess, Thomas Stöckl

ISBN 9783738657753
Herstellung und Verlag: BoD - Books on Demand,
Norderstedt, Germany

I speak from the heart Right from
the start.
I SPEAK FROM THE HEART RIGHT

FROM THE START.

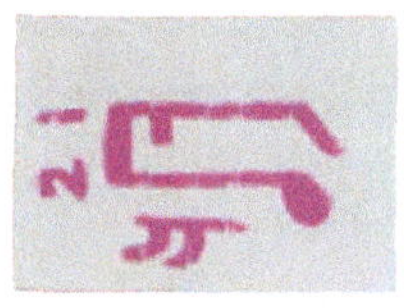
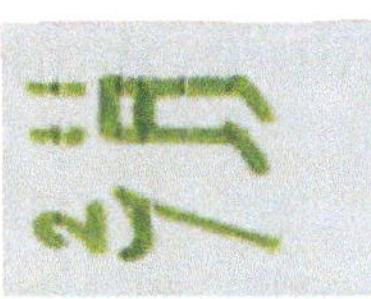
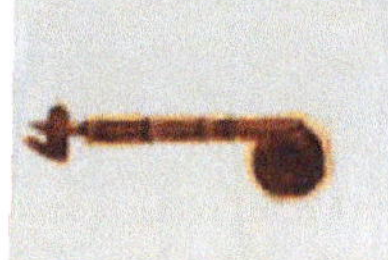
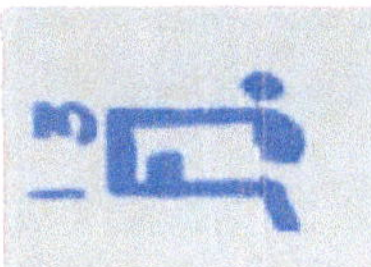
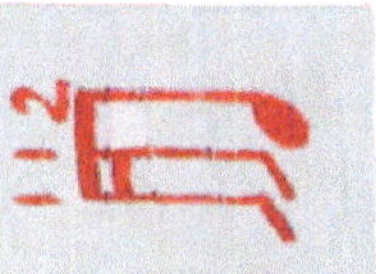
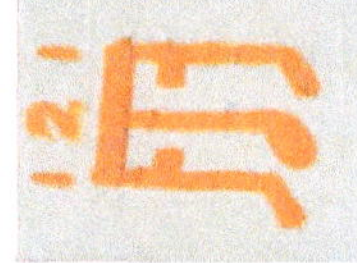
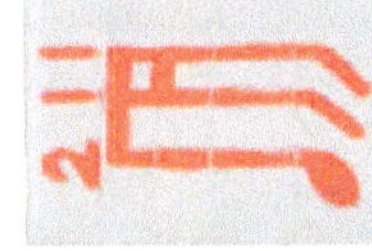
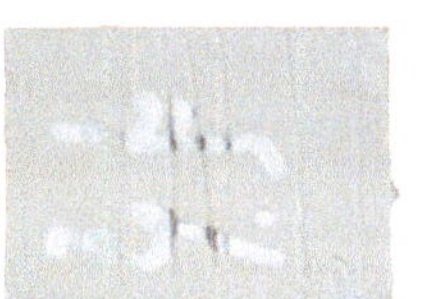
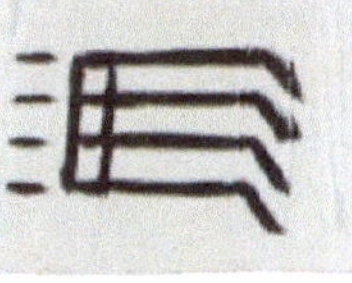
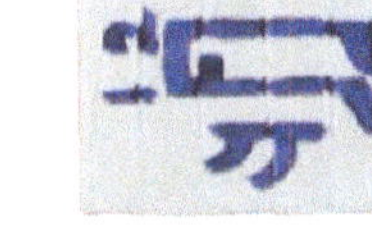
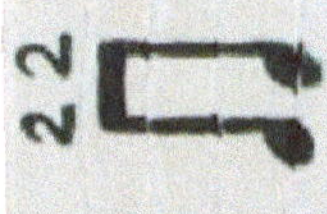

Edurhythmiccellsexcercise

(drumming with KENWOOD DENNARD, Boston)

1 BRAIN - VISION

4-Unit Rhythmic Cells Reading Excercise
This Exercise is designed to enable you to read common rhythms involving 16th note syncopation even if you start with NO reading ability at all.

Step One: Please set the metronome for 60 bpm…
Step Two: Please listen to the repeated click of the metronome. Please regard each click of the metronome as one unit of time.
Step Three: Please let one 16th note represent one unit of time.

I have organized the common rhythms involving 16th note syncopation into 12 4 unit ''rhythmic cells''. A rhythmic cell is a group of units of time where each unit of time is represented by a note value. A note value is defined as a note or a rest.
In the context of the Rhythmic Cells Excercise, here is what one sixteenth note looks like: Please note that in the Rhythmic Cells excercise, a sixteenth note consists of a solid note   head, a stem, and two beams. Now

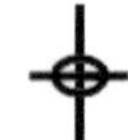

please identify each 16th note you see on the page as equal to one unit of time. Each time you see a 16th note, ease count the number ''one'' to identify it as one unit of time.
t may appear any one of four ways among the 12 essential Rhythmic Cells. It is comprised of 4 16thnotes.

***

Please look at Rhythmic Cell #1.
Can you identify the 16th notes in this rhythmic cell?
Please put your eye on each 16th note unit as it appears on the page.
Each time the metronome clicks, please put your eye on the first 16th note unit then on the next click put your eye on the second 16th note unit and every time the metronome clicks,   please put your eye on the next

subsequent 16th note unit.
Essential note value = a note or a rest
Let the16th note express that the quarter note = 4 16th note units

RHYTHMICCELLSCOUNTINGSYSTEM:

If you see ''1'' over a given note, please count ''1''. If you see ''2'' over
a given note, please count ''1,2''.
If you see ''3'' over a given note please count ''1,2,3''
And if you see ''4'' over a given note, please count ''1,2,3,4'' Please let one
click of the metronome equal one count.

CLAPPING ON ONE:
Please clap your hands together everytime you say the number one.
Please read the whole page as follows use the Rhythmic Cells Counting system and clap every time you say ''one''.

Start at 16th = 60 and increase to 16th = 120bqm metronome.

Edurhythmiccellsexcercise

(drumming with KENWOOD DENNARD, Boston) 1 BRAIN - VISION

4-Einheiten Rhythmic Cells Leseübung
Diese Übung wurde entwickelt um Sie in die Lage zu versetzen gewöhnliche Rhythmen, die 16tel Noten Synkope beinhalten zu erkennen, selbst wenn Sie über keinerlei Lesefähigkeiten verfügen sollten.

Schritt Eins: Setzen Sie bitte das Metronom auf 60bpm
Schritt Zwei: Hören Sie bitte auf den wiederkehrenden Klick des Metronoms. Bitte betrachten Sie jeden Klick als eine Zeiteinheit.
Schritt Drei: Lassen Sie bitte eine 16tel Note eine Zeiteinheit repräsentieren.

Ich habe Synkope 16tel Noten Rhythmen in 4 Einheiten von 12 Rhythmic Cells Einheiten eingeteilt. Eine Rhythmic Cell ist eine Gruppe von Zeiteinheit in der jede Zeiteinheit durch einen Notenwert repräsentiert wird. Ein Notenwert wird durch eine Note oder eine Pause definiert. Im Zusammenhang mit der Rhythmic Cell Übung sieht eine 16tel Note wie folgt aus: Bitte beachten Sie, dass in der Rhythmic Cell Übung eine 16tel Note aus einem soliden Notenkopf, einem Stil und zwei Fähnchen besteht. Nun identifizieren Sie bitte jede

16tel Note, die Sie in den Seiten sehen als eine Zeiteinheit. Jedes Mal, wenn Sie eine 16tel Note sehen, zählen Sie bitte "Eins" um sie als eine Einheit zu identifizieren. Dies für alle 4 Möglichkeiten der 12 Rhythmic Cells. ie beinhalten 4 Mal 16tel Noten.

***

Bitte schauen Sie Rhythmic Cell Nr. 1 an.
Können Sie die 16tel Noten in dieser Rhythmic Cell identifizieren?
Bitte richten Sie ihre Augen auf jede 16tel Noteneinheit wie sie auf der Seite steht. Bei jedem Klick des Metronoms richten Sie bitte Ihr Augenmerk auf die erste 16tel Noteneinheit, beim nächsten Klick richten Sie Ihr Augenmerk auf die zweite Noteneinheit und so weiter bei jedem Klick des Metronoms, bitte schauen Sie

auf die nächste 16tel Noteneinheit. Der wesentliche Notenwert = eine Note oder eine Pause.
Drücken Sie die 16tel Noten als Viertelnote aus = 4 16tel Noteneinheiten.

RHYTHMICCELLSZÄHLSYSTEM:
Wenn Sie eine "1" über einer Note sehen, zählen Sie bitte "1". Wenn Sie eine "2"

über einer Note sehen, zählen Sie bitte "1,2". Wenn Sie eine "3" über einer Note
sehen, zählen Sie bitte "1,2,3".
Und wenn Sie eine "4" über einer Note sehen, zählen Sie bitte "1,2,3,4" Bitte setzen Sie
einen Klick des Metronoms mit einer Zahl gleich.

KLATSCHÜBUNG:
Bitte klatschen Sie in die Hände immer dann, wenn Sie die Zahl eins sagen.
Bitte lesen Sie die ganzen Seite wie folgt mit dem Rhythmic Cells Zählsystem und klatschen Sie jedes Mal, wenn Sie "eins" sagen.
tarten Sie 16tel=60 und erhöhen Sie 16tel =120bqm mit dem Metronom.

Monochrome

Perfekter Moment

Es gibt etwas **Nichtmaterielles** in Musik und Bild, das dem Rationalen der menschlichen Psyche im Spirituellen, Mystischen, Nicht-sein entgegen steht. Eine Konkretisierung des Nichtmateriellen liegt im Unmöglichen und doch will es die Differenz unserer Differenz markieren.

Monochrome gehen in Extreme des Nichtseins.

Farbe ist eine unabdingbare Materie für Leben. Die Wiederbelebung eines leeren Raumes (eines weissen Raumes) ist wie "das Verdienst des Bildes, außerhalb des Endlichen, sich der Präzision zu entziehen" (Delacroix). Im Rausch der Farbe, wieder"belebt" findet das monochrome Bild den Zustand der Dinge und keine Geschichte der

Dinge.

Das monochrome Bild repräsentiert die gesamte Sensibilität einer Darstellung/Performance des Nichtmateriellen, der Differenz und ist Prozess und Selbsterfahrung zugleich. **Das Unendliche.**
s gibt keine endende Materie sowie der Künstler immer selbst auch ein nicht endendes Kunstwerk ist. Eine

unbekannte Sensibilität: die Seele empfinden ohne zu erklären.

Monochrome sind der Sprung eines Künstlers zugleich aus und in eine emotionale Welt. Das Monochrom ist die Projektion des Mystischen in die kollektive Imagination.
Monochrom heißt wahrhaft frei zu sein, durch die Farbe im "Raum" aufzugehen. Monochrom ist

der perfekte Moment.

Die Macht der Gefühle, also Emotionen sind -nach aktuellster Hirnforschung nun auch bestätigt-, die entscheidenden Antriebe unseres Tuns, emotionales Lernen eine beste Variante.
Die Lenkung oder Beherrschung eines Tones, die Raumbestimmung durch einen oder einige Töne ist genauso als

Komposition zu bezeichnen wie die Erstellung eines Bildes mit einer Farbe oder verschiedener Bilder mit mehreren Farben als Malerei.

Wie bei den monochromen Bildern die Atmosphäre des Raumes das Ziel ist und ihnen konsequenterweise der aktualisierte Raum folgt, so folgt dem mit unter gleichen Ton ein ebenso langes Schweigen.

Erlernen, Erkennen, Komponieren der Rhythmen lassen die Farbe der Rhythmen zu perfekten Momenten werden.

Setzen Sie sich dem Rausch der Farbe aus.

Verknüpfen Sie anschließend die Farbe mit der jeweiligen Rhythmic Cell und fliegen sie
avon...

Monochrome

perfectmoment

There is something **immaterial** in music and painting that is opposite the rational, spiritual, mystical, non-being. The concrete non-being is impossible to describe but will mark the difference of our difference.
Monochrome go to extremes of non-being.

Color is an indispensable material for life. The re-animation of the empty space (the white room) is "the merit of the picture in the withdraw from being final" (Delacroix).
Reanimate in exhilaration of color the Monochrome picture found the state of the thing and
not the history of it.

The Monochrome picture represent whole sensibility of representation/performance of immaterial, the difference, and represent the process and self awareness at the same time. The infinity.
There is no final material as well as an artist is always an artwork him/herself all time. An
unknown sensibility: soul feeling without explanation.

Monochromes are the artist's jump from and in an emotional world at the same time. The
Monochrome is the projection of the myth into the collective imagination.
Monochrome is being truly **free** in space of transition thru color.
Monochrome is the perfect moment.

The power of emotions -confirmed by actual neuroscience- is responsible for our drive and do's. Emotional learning is seen as one of the best variants.
Conducting or controlling a pitch, the determination of a space thru one or more pitches is defined as composing, painting a picture with one color or different pictures with more colors is defined as composing as

well.

Monochromes' goal is the atmosphere of space and consequently the given space follows so the same pitch is followed by same silence.

Learning, Recognizing, Composing the rhythms will grow the color of rhythms to perfect moments.

Expose yourself to the exhilaration of color.
Than bond the color with one of the rhythmic cells and fly....

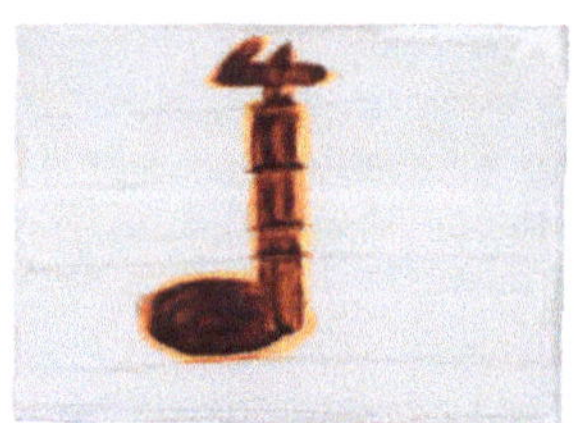

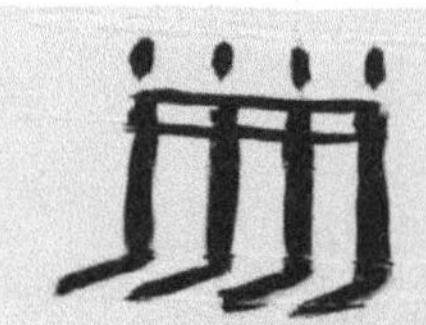

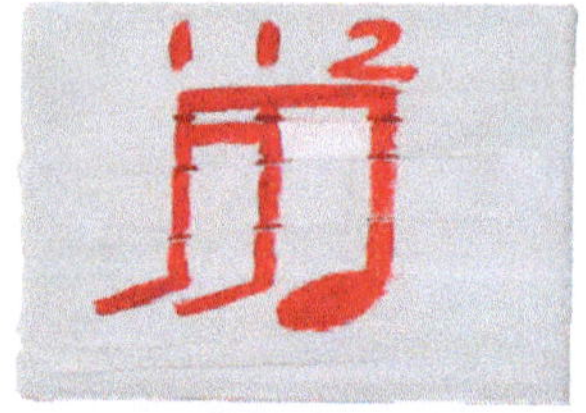

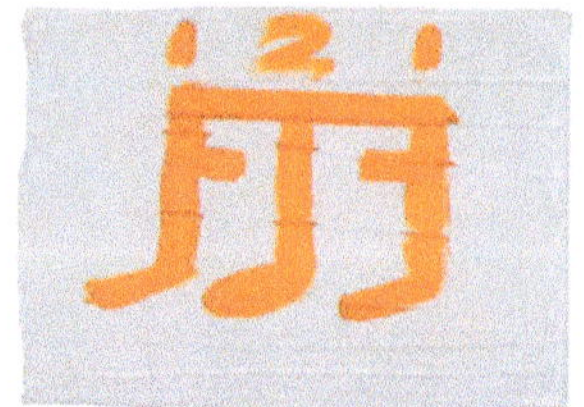

2 2

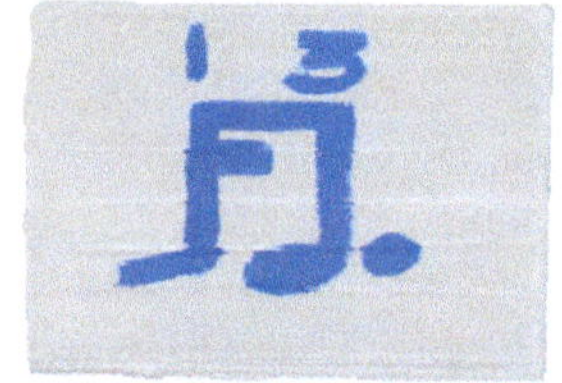

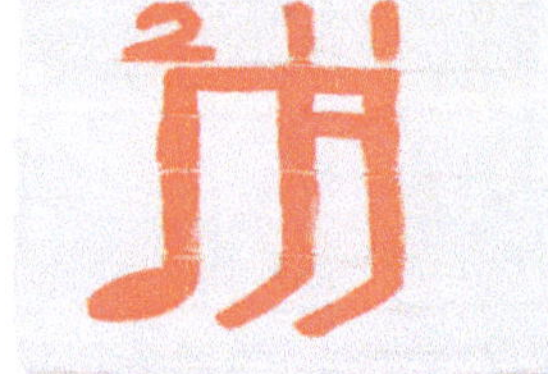

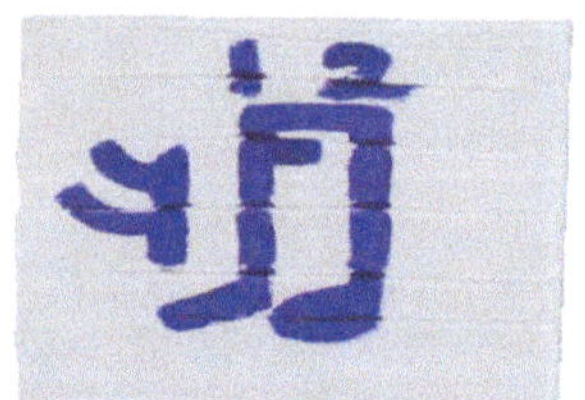

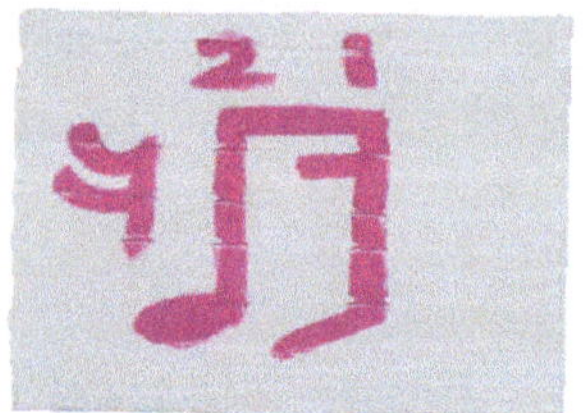

張黄

Alle Monochrome

71cm * 91 cm except green
rhythm2.2
81cm * 141cm

double framed ACRYL

on
RAW Terrané

AllRhythms

20cm * 20cm single

framed ACRYL on
Basics

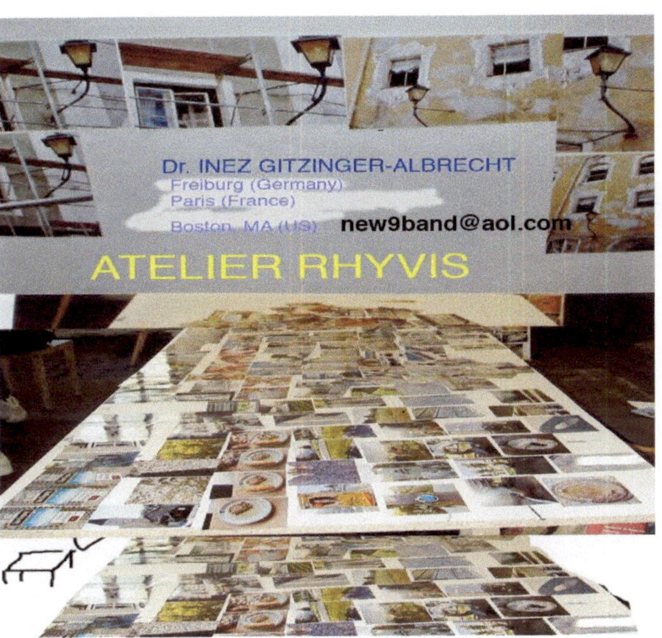

Dr. INEZ GITZINGER-ALBRECHT
Freiburg (Germany)
Paris (France)
Boston, MA (US)   new9band@aol.com
ATELIER RHYVIS